D0861033

Bowling Basics
A Step by Step Approach

Fourth Edition

Gerald P. Carlson

University of Southwestern Louisiana

E. Harold Blackwell

Lamar University

KENDALL/HUNT PUBLISHING COMPANY
4050 Westmark Drive   Dubuque, Iowa 52002

Contents

Preface

Bowling is a game for all ages and both sexes. It is considered to be one of the largest participation games in America today. Bowling is still one of the five basic life time sports promoted in Physical Education.

Bowling Basics presents the basic techniques and analyzes the basic fundamentals a student must learn in order to become a better bowler. History, values, terminology and game improvement techniques are detailed throughout the book. The basic fundamentals are presented in sequential order from selection of equipment to proper stance, types of grip, types of delivery, conversion of spares, analysis of errors and scoring. Each aspect of the game is clearly illustrated with photos and line drawings.

To assist the bowler in developing the finer aspects of the game, the appendicies contain skill development work sheets and scoring practice sheets.

Special appreciation is extended to the American Bowling Congress and the Women's International Bowling Congress who have granted permission to use concepts and excerpts from their publications.

Happy bowling and many high scores.

Gerald P. Carlson

E. Harold Blackwell

Acknowledgement

Appreciation is extended to Mr. Fred Nelson, Associate Professor and advanced bowling instructor in the department of Health and Physical Education at the University of Southwestern Louisiana for his contribution on "Ballistics of Bowling."

Chapter 1

History of Bowling

Early Developments

Bowling (in various forms) has been traced to articles found in the tomb of an Egyptian child buried in 5200 B.C. The primitive implements included nine pieces of stone at which a stone "ball" was rolled, the ball having first to roll through an archway made of three pieces of marble.

Another ancient discovery was the Polynesian games of ula maika, also utilizing pins and balls of stone. The stones were rolled at targets 60 feet away, which today still is one of the basic regulations of bowling.

Most historical accounts indicate that bowling was first introduced in Europe in 50 B.C. It was an Italian game called "Bocci."

Bowling at pins probably originated in ancient Germany, not as a sport but as a religious ceremony. The game was called Kegling. It was used by religious leaders in the Middle Ages in Germany to determine if a person was leading a "good" life. A man would place his pin (Kegel) at a distance and attempt to knock it down. A successful attempt would mean he was living a "good" life according to the religious principles.

Martin Luther is credited with setting nine as the ideal number of pins. The pins or Kegels were set up in a diamond pattern as opposed to the inverted pyramid pattern of today's modern tenpins.

Tracing history reveals that the game moved throughout Europe, the Scandinavian countries, and finally the United States. The earliest known reference to bowling at pins in America was made by author Washington Irving about 1818 in "Rip Van Winkle."

Although the game was being played throughout the world, rules were different almost everywhere, and even basic equipment was not the same. In fact, why and when the 10th pin was added from the European game of ninepins to the American game of tenpins still is a mystery.

Regardless of how the game came into being, it became so popular by the mid-19th century that indoor lanes were being built throughout Manhattan and the Bronx and on westward, in Syracuse, Buffalo, Cincinnati, Chicago, Milwaukee and other cities with large German populations.

Modern Developments

In 1988, under the direction of ABC, WIBC, USTBF, Brunswick and the Bowling Proprietors Association of America, bowling was introduced into the Olympic Games in Seoul Korea as an "Exhibition Sport." The FIQ will make a presentation to the International Olympic Committee to have bowling become a "medal status" sport in the Olympic Games after the year 2,000.

History of Bowling Organizations

ABC

In 1875, delegates from nine bowling clubs in New York and Brooklyn met in Germania Hall in the Bowery and organized the National Bowling Association. This was an attempt to bring some type of organized structure to the game.

Disagreement raged between East and West, principally the alignment of New York state bowlers against everyone else to the West. On September 9, 1895, the American Bowling Congress (ABC) was organized in Beethoven Hall in New York City. The breach was healed, rules and equipment standards were developed-and adhered to-and the game, as it finally was organized more than three-quarters of a century ago, has remained basically unchanged.

Basic concepts of the American Bowling Congress has remained unaltered since its inception in 1895. The settings have changed occasionally, and the ABC headquarters in the Southwest Milwaukee suburb of Greendale, Wisconsin, provide the finest facilities in history to service more than four million members.

The world's largest non-profit membership service organization exemplifies a stability on which its members and the rest of the bowling family can rely. In addition to numerous special services and programs available to its vast membership, ABC added a Seniors Program in 1963 and designed a complete set of services for the nation's senior citizens. The ABC National Seniors tournament for men 55 and older was initiated in 1964.

In 1966, a collegiate division was initiated by ABC to provide a program for the nation's college men while at the same time bridging the service gap between junior and adult competition. The national intercollegiate championships, sponsored by the Association of College Unions International (ACU-1) and AMF, Inc. are staged annually on ABC tournament lanes. Presently, the ABC and the Women's International Bowling Congress (WIBC) jointly sponsor the collegiate bowling program for men and women college students, faculties and staff.

The most spectacular of ABC's many services is the national championship tournament, the oldest and largest bowling event in the nation. A fixture on the sports scene since 1901, it is unrivaled as a participation or a non-participant spectacle. On lanes specially installed on alternate years by AMF and Brunswick in public arenas, 8,180 teams and 43,000 individuals have participated in one year. The tournament runs 12 to 16 hours daily for 60 to 90 consecutive days.

FIQ

The Federation Internationale des Quilleurs was created in 1952 and is the successor to the International Bowling Association formed in 1948. The FIQ is the world governing body for bowling.

USTBF

The United States Tenpin Bowling Federation was formed in June, 1989. The USTBF is the new national governing body for bowling in the United States.

WIBC

There are many colorful stories about when women began bowling in the United States. Oldtimers reminisce about the turn of the century, when their mothers or grandmothers sneaked in with (or without) their husbands to try out the bowling game. Tales are told of women being screened off from view behind partitions or drapes . . . or being allowed to bowl only when men are not using the lanes. Records show little activity until 1915, when Ellen Kelly, an avid bowler, formed the St. Louis Women's Bowling Association. By the fall of 1916, many had expressed interest in her ideas for a national group. Forty women from 11 cities met in 1916 and formed the national organization that became, after several name changes, the Women's International Bowling Congress.

The WIBC has developed into the largest sports organization in the world for women. The 40 pioneers, who met in 1916, set the pattern for today's over 4.2 million WIBC members, who bowl in more than 150,000 sanctioned leagues in more than 2,700 local associations in every state and several foreign countries.

YABA

The Young American Bowling Alliance, formerly called the American Junior Bowling Congress, coordinates bowling for youth in the United States. Since that historic day in 1964 when the AJBC shifted its headquarters from Chicago to Milwaukee and came under the guidance of ABC and WIBC, growth and improved services have better prepared this country's youth to become part of the world's largest participation sport.

Over a million young people bowling under the YABA banner are receiving the finest training available. The program began in Chicago in 1936 when a Tilden High School Teacher, Milt Raymer, now a member of the ABC Hall of Fame, organized an intramural bowling program.

Chapter 2
Values of Bowling

Physiological Values

The daily required tasks of our modern life style no longer provides us with the vigorous exercise we need to develop and maintain the so-called quantities of fitness. People are designed for various kinds of movement and physical activity. Since we are no longer required to perform the laborious tasks of yesteryear, our body is in need of other types of physical activity to help it develop properly and maintain a suitable level of fitness. Most medical authorities support the belief that exercise helps a person look, feel and work better. Various organs and systems of the body are stimulated through activity and as a result, function more effectively. One reason that bowling is such a popular sport today is that it does not require a high level of strength, power, speed and endurance. However, the sport of bowling does give a person a degree of satisfaction in fulfilling his need for physical activity.

In the analysis of the various motions executed in performing the necessary skills of bowling, one can clearly see the needed physical fitness components necessary for efficient execution of the movements of bowling. Some factors that affect a person's efficiency and skill in bowling are (1) the weight of the ball (2) coordination required for a proper approach and delivery (3) the repetitive stress and strain on particular muscle groups and (4) the duration of the activity (particularly in league bowling).

Psychological Values

In regards to the values of bowling, it is very important for a person to realize the psychological benefits of a physical activity, as well as the many physical benefits derived from regular participation. In today's society, there are many reasons for a person to "get away" from their everyday tasks and responsibilities. Stress and tension are two recognized factors that contribute to one's physical and mental problems. The physical and mental health of an individual depends on a person's ability to adapt to various situations.

As stated by Corbin, et al. "Stressors can be physical in nature or psychological. Physical stressors include heat, noise, and over crowding, malnutrition, climate, microorganisms, terrain, etc. Psychosocial stimuli are probably the most common stressors affecting humans. These include "life-change events," such as change in work hours or line of work, family illnesses, problems with superiors, death of relatives or friends, and increased responsibilities. In school, the pressures of grades, term papers, and oral presentation may induce stress."

Although it is basically impossible to avoid stressful situations, a person can adapt or "cope" with these unhealthy situations by planning his/her daily life in terms of broadening their interests and seeking diversions. This can partially be accomplished by regular participation in enjoyable physical activity. Bowling, or a participation activity, allows a person to "get away" and experience the mental relaxation that is important for healthy living.

Figure 2.1. Social interaction of bowling.

Social Values

As stated earlier in this chapter, bowling is an activity that is not too strenuous and does not demand a high level of physical skill to enjoy. It is a common fact that people select activities in which they can succeed. Bowling is an activity that does not have to be highly competitive. A person can "win" simply by deriving enjoyment from participation. Bowling gives a person the needed opportunity to be with others and enjoy the many benefits derived from being around friends. League bowling gives a person the unique and valuable opportunity to make friends and gain social competence from this experience.

Recreational Values

Recreation is considered a worthwhile, socially acceptable, leisure experience providing immediate and inherent satisfaction to the individual who voluntarily participates in an activity. In the true sense of the term, recreation provides an individual with many sociological and emotional satisfactions.

Today's society is an age of leisure. Leisure time is becoming more and more prevalent in our lives. It is very important that a person makes constructive use of his/her leisure. The values of recreation are immense, and are determined by the individual's motivating factors.

Recreation, when properly planned, can contribute to a person's well-being by:

1. providing a "get away" from harmful stress
2. relieving excessive tension
3. providing for needed physical activity
4. helping in the development of social competencies

The basic physical fitness components necessary for the optimum development of bowling skills are:

1. *Muscular Strength*—particularly the muscle groups of the upper arms and shoulders. As a muscle is strengthened so is its movement efficiency. This necessary efficiency of movement allows a person to more readily develop the smooth and coordinated approach and delivery, the two basic fundamentals of bowling
2. *Muscular Endurance*—particularly in muscle groups of the upper arm, shoulder and legs-this allows an individual to carry out activity without undue fatigue. The authors of this text have observed on hundreds of occasions the effect of prolonged bowling on a person's bowling ability. Many bowlers begin to lose effectiveness after only one game. This undue fatigue is caused by lack of muscular endurance. Since the acquisition of bowling skills requires repetitions of skill practice, it is highly advantageous for a person to have good muscular endurance. Muscular endurance also allows a person to maintain good form and technique during the later stages of a match.

Chapter 3

Terminology

A

ABC

American Bowling Congress (Men's organization)

AJBC

American Junior Bowling Congress (Boy's and girl's organization)

Alley

A bowling lane or a bowling center

All Events

The total of games bowled by an individual in one tournament, usually three games in the team event, three in doubles and three in singles. Sometimes the totals for the three events by the five members of one team.

Anchorman

Last bowler on a team. Usually the best bowler.

Approach

The area behind the foul line on which a player takes his steps prior to delivering the ball. At least 15′ long.

Arrows

Sighting targets imbedded in the lane to help a player align the starting position on the approach with the ball path to the pocket.

B

Baby Split

The 2-7 *or* 3-10 split.

Backup

A ball that curves left to right for a right-hander and right to left for a left-hander.

Backswing

The path of the arm behind the body during the next to last step in the delivery.

Ballistics

The study of the flight characteristics of projectiles as it applies to bowling.

Bedposts

The 7-10 split.

Blind

The score given for a missing bowler. The score is usually 90% of the person's average.

Blow

Failure to convert a spare. An error, miss.

Bridge

Distance between finger holes on the ball.

Brooklyn

A right-handed bowler hitting to the left of the head pin and a left-handed bowler hitting to the right of the head pin. Also called a crossover or Jersey.

Buck

A game under 200; i.e., A buck seventy six is a 176 game.

Bucket

The 2-4-5-8 or 3-5-6-9 pin leaves

C

Channel

Dropoff area on each side of the lane. Called the gutter.

Channel Ball

A ball rolled in the channel. A gutter ball.

Cherry

Knocking down the front pin of a spare and leaving the other pins standing. Also called a chop.

Chop

See Cherry

Convert

When you successfully make your spare.

Count

The number of pins knocked down on the first ball.

Creeper

A ball rolled very slowly.

Crossover

See Brooklyn

Curve

A ball that has a wide sweeping arc. The ball moves first toward the outside of the lane and then curves toward the inside.

D

Deuce

200 average or 200 game.

Dead Ball
> A poorly rolled ball that has little or no spin or "action" and doesn't knock down as many pins as it should.

Dead Mark
> A tenth frame strike or spare; no bonus is allowed.

Double
> Two strikes in succession.

Double Pinochle Split
> The 4-7-6-10

Dutch 200
> A game of exactly 200 made by alternating strikes and spares.

E

Error
> Failure to convert a spare. Also called a blow, miss or open.

F

FIQ
> The Federation Internationale des Quilleurs is the world governing body for bowling.

Fast Lane
> A lane which holds down the hook. The lane is slippery and does not allow the ball the necessary coefficient of friction to track properly.

Fill Ball
> Last ball strike in the tenth frame.

Foul
> Touching or going beyond the foul line when delivering the ball.

Foul Line
> The line separating the approach and the lane.

Frame
> One-tenth of a game. Each large box on a scoresheet indicates a frame.

G

Graveyard
> A low scoring lane.

Grinder
> A powerful hook or curve ball.

Gutter
> See channel.

Gutter Ball
>See channel ball.

H

Handicap
>A means of adjusting scores so as to place teams or individuals with varying degrees of skills on as equitable basis as possible for their competition against each other.

Head Pin
>The No. 1 Pin

High Board
>An expanded or loose board in a lane which can cause a ball to veer from its path.

High Hit
>A ball hitting almost solidly on the head pin.

Holding Lane
>See fast lane.

Hook
>A left break ball for a right-hand bowler.

K

Kegler
>German word for bowler derived from the word Kegel (pin).

Kickbacks
>Side partitions between lanes at the pit end.

King Pin
>The No. 5 pin.

L

Lane
>The sixty foot area between the foul line and the head pin.

Lead Off
>The first bowler in a team lineup.

Leave
>The pins that remain standing after the first ball delivery.

Light Hit
>A ball that barely hits the pocket.

Line
>A game of ten frames. Also refers to the path a ball travels.

Lofting
>Tossing the ball far out beyond the foul line. Normally caused by a late release.

M

Mark

Getting a strike or spare.

Miss

Failure to convert a spare leave. Also called a blow or error.

Mixer

A ball which hits the pins lightly, causing the pins to ricochet, usually results in a strike.

N

Nose Hit

A ball that hits full on the head pin. Also called a high hit.

O

Open

A frame in which the player fails to strike or spare.

P

Perfect Game

A 300 score. Strikes in all ten frames. Twelve consecutive strikes.

Pin

The object which the bowler is trying to knock down.

Pin Bowler

A bowler who aims (visually) at the pin when delivering the ball.

Pin Deck

The area where the pins are placed.

Pitch

The angle at which the finger holes are bored in a ball.

Pocket

The area between the 1-3 pins for a right-hander and the area between the 1-2 pins for the left-hander.

R

Railroad

Term associated with the 4-6 and 7-10 splits. Also called a double pinochle split.

Return

The track or rails on which the ball rolls back to a player.

S

Sandbagging

Deliberately holding down a league average in order to receive an advantage of a higher handicap in league or tournament play.

Scratch Bowler

A bowler who has no handicap.

Series

Usually three games or more in a league or tournament.

Sleeper

A pin hidden behind another.

Sour Apple

The 5-7 pin leave.

Span

Distance between thumb and finger holes.

Spare

Knocking down all ten pins with two balls in a frame.

Split

Combinations of pins left standing after first delivery with a pin down immediately ahead or between them. The headpin must be down to record a split.

Spot Bowler

A bowler who uses the finders or spots as their primary target. Opposite of pin bowler.

Stork Bowler

Keeping the legs straight instead of bending into the slide during the delivery.

Strike

Knocking down all the pins with the first ball of a frame.

Strike Out

To get three strikes in the tenth and final frame.

T

Tap

A pin left standing on an apparent good strike hit.

Thin Hit

See light hit.

Turkey

Three consecutive strikes.

U

USTBF
> The United States Tenpin Bowling Federation is the new governing body for all bowling in the United States. It coordinates the efforts of ABC, WIBC and YABA.

W

Washout
> The 1-2-4-10 leave for a right-hander; the 1-3-6-7 leave for a left hander.

Water Ball
> A ball delivered poorly.

WIBC
> Women's International Bowling Congress.

Working Ball
> A ball with much spin action which drives into the pocket. Also called a mixer.

Y

YABA
> The Young American Bowling Alliance, formerly called the American Junior Bowling Congress.

Chapter 4

Etiquette and Rules

Every sport has a code of etiquette and rules which governs play and improves the conduct of the game. Bowling is no exception. The following are most important to help make the game more enjoyable.

Etiquette

Proper conduct, sportsmanship, consideration of others and plain common sense arc important to succeed and to enjoy bowling. The following rules of etiquette should be practiced by bowlers:

1. Be prepared to take your regular turn on the lanes.
2. Generally, the person on the right bowls first;
   - don't step on the approach until right of way is determined
   - don't wait for bowlers several lanes away
   - the spare bowler will go first
3. Take your time, but don't waste time by posing to wait until everyone else is off the approaches.
4. Stay on your own approach at all times.
   Step back off the approach after making each delivery.
5. Do not "double ball" (using 2 different balls during a game).
6. Do not use another player's equipment without permission.
7. Good bowling requires concentration. When a player is ready to bowl, give the bowler the courtesy of making the shot without interference. Save the kidding for the bench or the locker room.
8. Be ready to bowl, but wait until the pinsetting machine has completed its cycle and the sweep bar is raised before rolling the ball.
9. Respect the equipment. Getting the ball out on the lane is good, but lofting is bad for the lane, and it won't help your game. Wear regulation shoes so it doesn't ruin the approach and allows you to slide.
10. Play the game to win, but be gracious if you are on the short end of the score at the end of the game.
11. Control your emotions on the lanes. Kicking the ball rack or using foul language doesn't help anyone.
12. Do not tell others about their errors, concentrate on your own game.
13. Observe common courtesy toward other bowlers at all times. This favor will also be returned to you which helps makes bowling enjoyable to everyone.

Scoring the Game

The game of bowling shall consist of ten frames. Each player shall bowl two balls in each of the first nine frames except when a strike is made. A player who scores a strike in the tenth frame shall deliver three balls. The player receives a one ball bonus for a spare and a two ball bonus for a strike.

Legal Delivery

1. A ball is legally delivered when it leaves the bowler's possession and crosses the foul line into playing territory.
2. A bowling ball must be delivered entirely by manual means and shall not incorporate any device either in the ball or affixed to it which is either detached at time of delivery or is a moving part in the ball during delivery. Any person who has had his hand or major portion thereof amputated, may use special equipment to aid in grasping and delivering the ball providing the special equipment is in lieu of the amputee's hand.

Pinfall—Legal

Every ball delivered by the player shall count unless declared a dead ball. Pins must then be respotted after the cause for declaring such a dead ball has been removed:

1. Pins which are knocked down by another pin or pins rebounding in play from the side partition, rear cushion or sweep bar when they are at rest on the pin deck prior to sweeping dead wood are counted as pins down.
2. If when rolling at a full setup or in order to make a spare, it is discovered immediately after the ball has been delivered that one or more pins are improperly set, although not missing, the ball and resulting pinfall shall be counted. It is each player's responsibility to determine if the setup is correct. The bowler shall insist that any pins incorrectly set be reported before delivering his ball, otherwise it is implied that the setup is satisfactory. No change in the position of any pins which are left standing can be made after the previous delivery in order to make a spare, unless the pin setter has moved or misplaced any pin after the previous delivery and prior to the bowling of the next ball.
3. Pins which are knocked down or displaced by a fair ball, and remain lying on the lane or in the gutters, or which lean so as to touch the kickbacks or side partitions are termed deadwood, counted as pins down, and must be removed before the next ball is bowled.
4. If a bowler knowingly makes a legal delivery while there is dead wood on the lane or in the gutters, and his ball comes in contact with such dead wood before leaving the lane surface, then the bowler shall receive a score of zero for that delivery.

Pinfall—Illegal

When any of the following incidents occur the ball counts as a ball rolled, but pins knocked down shall not count:

1. When pins are knocked down or displaced by a ball which leaves the lane before reaching the pins.
2. When a ball rebounds from the rear cushion.
3. When pins come in contact with the body, arms or legs of a human pinsetter and rebound.

4. A standing pin which falls when it is touched by mechanical pinsetting equipment, or when dead wood is removed, or is knocked down by a human pinsetter, shall not count and must be replaced on the pinspot inscribed on the pin deck where it originally stood before delivery of the ball.
5. A pin which is bowled off the lane, rebounds and remains standing on the lane must be counted as a pin standing.
6. If in delivering the ball a foul is committed, any pins knocked down by such delivery shall not be counted.

Dead Ball

A ball shall be declared dead if any of the following occur, in which case the ball shall not count, the pins must be respotted after the cause for declaring such dead ball has been removed and player shall be required to rebowl:

1. If, after the player delivers his ball and attention is immediately called to the fact that one or more pins were missing from the setup.
2. When a human pinsetter removes or interferes with any pin or pins before they stop rolling or before the ball reaches the pins.
3. When a player bowls on the wrong lane or out of turn.
4. When a player is interfered with by a pinsetter, another bowler, a spectator, or moving object as the ball is being delivered and before delivery is completed, player must then and there accept the resulting pinfall or demand that the pins be respotted.
5. When any pins at which he is bowling are moved or knocked down in any manner, as the player is delivering the ball and before the ball reaches the pins.
6. When a player's ball comes in contact with any foreign obstacle.

Conceded Pins

No pins may be conceded. Only those pins actually knocked down or moved entirely off the playing surface of the lane as a result of the legal delivery of the ball by the player may be counted. Every frame must be completed at the time the player is bowling in his/her regular order.

Fouls—Defined

A foul is committed with no pinfall being credited to the player although the ball counts as a ball rolled, when a part of the bowler's person encroaches upon or goes beyond the foul line and touches any part of the lane, equipment or building during or after executing a legal delivery. A ball is in play and a foul may be called after the legal delivery has been made until the same or another player is on the approach in position to make a succeeding delivery.

If the player commits a foul, which is apparent to both captains or one or more members of each of the opposing teams competing in a league or tournament on the same pair of lanes where the foul is committed, or to the official scorer or tournament official, and should the foul judge or umpire through negligence fail to see it committed or an ABC approved automatic foul detecting device fails to record it, a foul shall nevertheless be declared and so recorded.

Deliberate Foul

When a player deliberately fouls to benefit by the calling of a foul, the player shall receive a zero pinfall for that delivery and shall not be allowed any further deliveries in that frame.

Foul Counts as Ball Bowled

A foul ball shall be recorded as a ball bowled by the player, but any pins bowled down when a foul is committed shall not be counted. When the player fouls upon delivering the first ball of a frame, all pins knocked down must be respotted, and only those pins knocked down by the second ball may be counted. If all pins are bowled down with the second ball, after fouling with the first, it shall be scored as a spare. When less than ten pins are bowled down on the second ball after fouling on the first, it shall be scored as an error. A player who fouls when delivering the second ball of a frame shall be credited with only those pins knocked down with the first ball, provided no foul was committed when the first ball was delivered. When a bowler fouls during the delivery of the first ball in the tenth frame and bowls down all ten pins with the second ball (making a spare) a third ball is bowled and credit is given for a spare plus the pins bowled down with the third ball. When a player fouls while delivering the third ball in the tenth frame, only those pins bowled down in delivering the first two balls shall be counted.

Chapter 5
Equipment

One of the reasons bowling is a popular life time sport is that no specialized equipment needs to be purchased by the beginner. All bowling establishments provide balls and shoes for a minimal rental fee. Standards for lanes, pins, and balls are certified by ABC therefore eliminating those decisions by the beginning bowler. As a person progresses in skill and appreciation for bowling, personalized equipment can be purchased for a reasonable amount.

Figure 5.1. Assorted bowling equipment.

Clothing

It is not necessary to have a special uniform to bowl. You should dress comfortably with loose fitting clothing that permits freedom of movement. Restrictive clothing may hinder bending, sliding and arm action.

Bowling shoes are designed to allow you to start and stop properly. When purchasing your own shoes, check to see that the composition of the sole is correct. The sole of the left shoe for a right hand bowler is leather to permit the slide on the last step. The sole of the right shoe is made of rubber with a leather lip which allows for traction at the start of the delivery. Rental shoes at bowling establishments have leather soles to accommodate either a right or left handed bowler.

Ball Selection

Like most sporting equipment, there are also technical specifications for size and weight of a bowling ball. After drilling, a regulation bowling ball shall not weigh more than 16 pounds. Balls over 10 pounds are permitted top and bottom balance variance of 3 ounces, and side to side or front to back variances of 1 ounce. For balls under 10 pounds, the imbalance may not exceed 3/4 ounce. Most bowling balls are made of either hard rubber or plastic.

The circumference of the ball shall be 27.002 inches maximum, 26.704 inches minimum. The diameter shall be 8.595 inches maximum and 8.500 inches minimum.

Selection of the bowling ball is very important. Most men select a ball approaching the 16 pound maximum. Because strength is a factor, women generally select a ball in the 10, 12, 14 pound range. Eight, 9, 10 pound balls are available for young people and those with physical handicaps.

The key is that the ball feels comfortable and can be gripped and swung without excessive strain. If the ball is constantly dropped at the foul line, the ball is either too heavy or improperly delivered. If your score is lower in the third game the ball is probably too heavy.

The most important aspect of selecting a ball is getting a span that fits the bowler's hand comfortably. The holes should be large enough so the thumbs and fingers do not stick. Also it must not be too loose which may cause the ball to drop, cause excess strain in gripping or blisters. You will not be able to hold the ball properly if the span is either too narrow or too wide. To check the recommended conventional grip, apply the following steps: (See fig. 5.2, 5.3)

1. Insert your thumb to its full length in the ball.
2. Lay the fingers across, not into their respective holes.
3. The crease of the second joint should extend 1/4 inch beyond the nearest edge of the finger holes.
4. If the joints do not reach the edge, the span is too wide.
5. If they go more than half way beyond the center of the holes, the span is too narrow.

Another check point is to insert the thumb and fingers. Let the ball hang from the hand. The space between the ball and the hand should be wide enough to insert a lead pencil without being too loose or tight.

Figure 5.2. Measuring hole length.

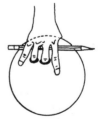

Figure 5.3. Measuring grip.

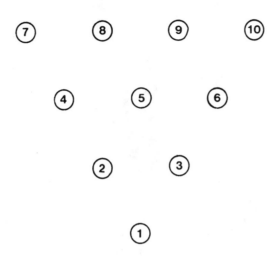

Figure 5.4. Pin placement and numbers.

Pins

An ABC approved pin is 15 inches high. The diameter at the base is 2 inches and approximately 4 3/4 inches at the widest point (4 1/2 inches above the base). Most pins are made of laminated hard maple and fitted with a plastic base and covered with a plastic coating. Synthetic or nonwood pins also have been developed. Approved weight range for plastic coated wood pins is 3 pounds 2 ounces to 3 pounds 10 ounces. Approved synthetic or non-wood pins range in weight from 3 pounds 4 ounces to 3 pounds 6 ounces.

The pins are set up on the end of the lane, 3 feet from the front of the head pin (#1) to the pit area. Pins are placed 12 inches apart, measured from the center of the pin. Dots are placed on the lane to indicate position of the pins. Pins are arranged in four rows and they are numbered from left to right, from front to back. (See fig. 5.4)

Lane

Bowling lane specifications are standardized and they are inspected and certified annually by ABC to assure uniform playing conditions. The lane bed is constructed of 1 inch wide, 3 inches thick, hard maple on the first third of the lane and pindeck and pine on the remaining portion of the lane. The lane is covered with a high gloss wax. The wax affects the amount of hook or curve due to rotation or delivery of the ball.

The lane is divided into a variety of areas. Each is presented to familiarize the bowler with the entire area.

Approach

The approach is a level runway a minimum of 15' from the foul line toward the seats. This is where the stance, approach, release and follow through are made. (See fig. 5.5)

Foul Line

The foul line is a horizontal mark separating the approach from the lane. (See fig. 5.5)

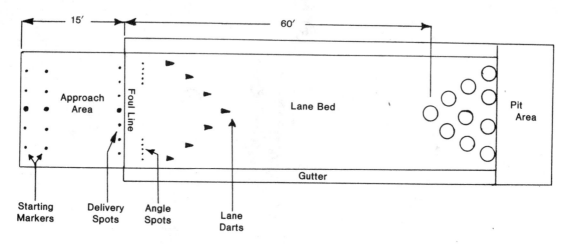

Figure 5.5. Lane diagram.

Lane Bed

The lane bed is the bowling surface that extends 60′ from the foul line to the center of the head pin (#1) and 3′ from the front of the head pin (#1) to the pit area. The maximum width of the lane is 42 inches, the minimum width is 41 inches. The bowling lane is level so no area is more than 40/1000 of an inch higher or lower than any other section. (See fig. 5.5)

Pit

The pit is located directly behind the pins. It collects pins that have been knocked down. It is approximately 4 inches below the lane bed and no less than 30 inches deep from rear cushion to end of the lane. (See fig. 5.5)

Lane Markings

All lanes have two sets of 5 *starting markers* located 12 and 15 feet behind the foul line which help the bowler find the correct starting position which is based upon length of the bowler's stride. (See fig. 5.5)

There are 7 *delivery spots* in front of the foul line to help the bowler check the accuracy of the ball. (See fig. 5.5)

There are 10 *angle spots* 7 feet beyond the foul line to help the bowler establish the correct angle for the path of the ball. (See fig. 5.5)

There are 7 *lane darts* arranged scientifically in the lane bed starting 13 feet 10 inches beyond the foul line. These darts are also used by the bowler to establish the correct angle for the path of the ball. (See fig. 5.5)

Chapter 6

Basic Fundamentals

Upon observing bowlers, you will find that there is no perfect style or form for bowling. However, there are basic fundamentals that all bowlers must learn. Once these fundamentals are learned, only slight modifications will need to be made to help the bowler improve. In this chapter the basic fundamentals will be presented in the sequence in which they occur.

Removing Ball from Ball Return

The object of taking the ball off ball return is to keep the hand from ever being caught between the balls. The ball should be removed with both hands. Place the hands on opposite sides of the ball, away from incoming balls. (Fig. 6. 1) This prevents the fingers from getting crushed. Do not pick the ball up with the fingers in the holes. Fingers should not be inserted until the stance has been taken and the approach is ready to be made.

Cradle the Ball

Before inserting your fingers in the ball and while finding your starting position the ball should be cradled in your hands. (Fig. 6.2) For a right handed bowler the ball rests in the left hand and is supported on the side by the right hand. The ball may rest next to the body.

Figure 6.1. Removing ball from ball return.

Figure 6.2. Cradle ball.

Starting Position

To become proficient at bowling it is important to establish a consistent starting position and a comfortable stance. To select the correct starting position the procedures listed below should be followed:

1. Start at the foul line facing the approach area
2. Place the heels 2 inches in front of the foul line
3. Take 4 1/2 brisk steps forward
4. Either look at the dots or the ball return to determine where you are
5. Turn and face the pins, you should be approximately at your starting point
6. Take several practice approaches. If you end up over the foul line, start back further. If you stop before the foul line, move closer.

For the right handed bowler the starting point should be to the right of the center dot. The right foot should line up directly above the board that has the 2nd dot to the right of the center. This should be in line with the second arrow on the lane from the right hand gutter. This is the common line for a strike ball. (Fig. 6.3)

Stance

After finding your starting position it is important to establish a stance that is comfortable and natural. The following are several techniques that will help to develop a proper stance: (Fig. 6.4)

1. The ball may be held close to the body or away
2. The height of the ball can be anywhere from the waist to the shoulder whichever is most comfortable.
3. Keep the shoulders square, level, and parallel to the foul line

Figure 6.3. Proper starting position.

Figure 6.4. Proper stance.

Figure 6.5. Proper wrist position.

4. Thumb in ball toward an 11 o'clock position
5. Wrist should be fairly firm and straight, do not bend back or cup
6. Bend knees slightly
7. Weight should be transferred to the left foot for a right handed bowler (4 step approach).
8. The feet should be fairly close together with the left foot slightly ahead.

Not all of these suggestions will work for everyone. Try them, modify them and use what works *best* for you. Variations are acceptable provided they are comfortable and help you to bowl better.

Wrist Position

The wrist should be straight and firm as the first step and push away is made. The wrist should not be bent back or cupped around the ball. Concentration is essential for proper wrist position. A wrist support may be beneficial in assuring this. (Fig. 6.5)

Grip

A bowler must use a ball which fits the hand to attain any degree of enjoyment and success. Most important, the grip should be natural and comfortable. There should not be any strain on the thumb, fingers or wrist. The majority of bowlers use one of three basic grips; conventional, fingertip, or semi-fingertip.

Conventional Grip

To check for the conventional grip, insert the thumb to its full length in the ball. Then lay fingers across, not into, their respective holes. The crease of the second joint should extend about one-fourth inch beyond the nearest edge of the finger holes. If the joints do not reach the edge, the span is too wide. If they go more than halfway beyond the center of the holes, the span is too narrow. (Fig. 6.6)

Figure 6.6. Conventional grip.   **Figure 6.7.** Fingertip grip.   **Figure 6.8.** Semi-fingertip grip.

Beginning bowlers should use the conventional grip because it provides a firmer hold with the fingers. It also gives the bowler a more secure feeling about having full control of the ball. The conventional grip allows the bowler to hold more of the ball, this providing the feeling of a secure release.

The conventional grip does not allow for exceptional lifting action, but it does provide the bowler the ability to hook the ball into the strike pocket. Upon becoming a more experienced bowler, the change to a fingertip or semi-fingertip grip can be made.

Fingertip Grip

The ball is supported only by the first joint of the bowlers fingers. The thumb is inserted all the way into the ball. When the bowler's fingers are extended over the finger holes, the first joint crease should extend slightly over the inner edge of the hole. This provides a comfortable fingertip grip. The fingertip allows for the greatest leverage at the release point, thus giving increased lift and or rotation. The wide span could present problems for the beginner bowler, but for the advanced bowler a comfortable fitting fingertip grip will provide an easily controlled release (Fig. 6.7)

Semi-Fingertip Grip

The thumb is inserted all the way into the ball. The fingers are inserted into the finger holes anywhere between the first and second joint. Since the depth of the fingers could vary in a semifingertip, it is possible that a bowler may get a different feel or different release occasionally. (Fig. 6.8)

A semi-fingertip grip might be advisable for the bowler who is not comfortable in a full fingertip grip. A fingertip grip is recommended over a semi-fingertip grip.

Approach

The approach is the method of advancing toward the foul line to deliver the ball. There are three basic approaches; the three, four and five step approach. Seldom is the three step approach taught because it does not allow sufficient time to complete the pendulum swing before reaching the foul line. Only the four and five step approaches will be presented.

Four Step Approach

The four step approach allows for the most natural rhythmic body movement during the delivery, increases accuracy and reduces fatigue. Coordination of the foot and arm action in the delivery is one of the most important parts of the mechanics of bowling. It is important to start slow and move progressively faster as you reach the foul line. The total movement involves taking a short step with the right foot. This may be a short shuffle step of no more than 6" to 12". The second and third steps are fairly evenly spaced and in a progressively faster rhythm. The fourth step is actually a slide. At the finish, the toe of the left foot should be pointing straight ahead and should finish within 6 inches of the foul line.

To insure starting on the proper foot (right) when you take your original stance, shift the weight to the left foot. That way, the only foot you can move first will be the right foot.

The following procedures should be followed in learning the four step approach:

1. *Push Away*—On the first step the ball is pushed away from the body. The motion should be forward and downward. The ball should be pushed forward as far as your right foot moves forward. (See Fig. 6.9)
2. *Down Swing*—On the second step the left hand is released from the ball and is used for balance. The weight of the ball and gravity pull the ball downward to a position at the side of the leg close to the body. Keep wrist firm and straight. (Fig. 6.10)
3. *Back Swing*—On the third step (right foot) the pendulum motion of the ball carries the ball backwards to a position that should not exceed the height of the hip. At this point, the body should be leaning forward and the knees should be slightly bent. This causes the increase in acceleration toward the foul line. (Fig. 6.1 1)
4. *Forward Swing*—On the fourth step (left foot, slide) the weight of the ball swings forward in a straight line toward the foul line.

For proper timing the ball and foot must reach the foul line at the same time. At this moment the weight is on the ball of the left foot, the shoulders should be parallel to the foul line, the left toe should be pointed straight ahead, the knees bent, the body is leaning forward, and the eyes are focusing on the spot you want the ball to travel over. (Fig. 6.12)

In review, think of the four step approach as four different movements. Count them out! 1. Simultaneously step with the right foot and push the ball forward and downward. 2. Simultaneously step with the left foot and swing the ball downward next to the body. 3. Simultaneously step with the right foot and swing the ball backward to approximately hip height. 4. Simultaneously slide the left foot forward and swing the ball toward the foul line. At first the four count-four step approach may seem mechanical. With practice and time, a rhythm of delivery will be established.

Figure 6.9. Push away.

Figure 6.10. Down swing.

Figure 6.11. Back swing.

Figure 6.12. Forward swing.

Five Step Approach

The five step approach is basically the same as the four step approach. The difference is that in the five step approach, the first step is with the left foot. The ball is not pushed away until the start of the forward movement of the right foot as in the four step approach. This pre-movement of an extra step can be a relaxing motion for the bowler.

1. 1st step—left foot shuffle
2. 2nd step—push away
3. 3rd step—downward swing
4. 4th step—Backswing
5. 5th step—Forward Swing

Release

Upon reaching the foul line the ball is released. The ball is released by the thumb first, generally from an 11 o'clock position. The thumb comes out of the ball with the wrist fairly firm, the fingers automatically lift the ball over the foul line. This lift also gives the ball rotation. The ball should contact the floor beyond the foul line. (Fig. 6.13)

Follow Through

Once the ball has been released it is important to have a follow through. This is the continuation of the upward arm action after the ball has been released. The follow through should be kept in line with the intended target and should be waist high or above. You should end up with your right hand in front of the right shoulder. (Fig. 6.14)

Figure 6.13. Release.

Figure 6.14. Follow through.

Delivery

The delivery involves the action and path the ball takes as it moves down the lane towards the pins. There are four basic deliveries: hook ball, straight ball, curve ball and backup ball.

Straight Ball

The straight ball is used by some beginners. Because there is a large amount of deflection and a poor angle to the 1-3 pocket it is considered a poor strike ball. Consistency in delivery is difficult with a straight ball because of lane conditions. A straight ball is delivered with the thumb in a 12 o'clock position and the ring and middle fingers are at a 6 o'clock position. Bowlers with weak wrists generally believe they can support the ball better this way. Many end up dropping the thumb to the right causing a backup ball. The path of the ball generally passes over the 2nd arrow from the right hand gutter and makes a straight line toward the 1-3 pocket. If you roll a straight ball you are only a slight hand movement away from throwing a hook ball. A slight rotation at the start or release will affect the change. (See figure 6.15 for the path of a straight ball).

Hook Ball

The hook is the best delivery to learn because it causes greater pin action, cuts down on deflection and provides more strikes. To roll a hook ball, the ball should be held as if you were shaking hands with someone. Or, place the thumb at a 10–11 o'clock position with the ring and middle fingers at a 4-5 o'clock position. The hook action results from the lifting action of the fingers from the 4 or 5 o'clock position beneath the ball. The wrist is kept straight and the fingers remain in the same position throughout the entire approach. The release causes the lifting and rotation action on the follow through. The path of a hook ball passes over the 2nd arrow from the right hand gutter, rolls straight and in the last 10-15 feet, hooks into the 1-3 pocket. The path of the hook ball is shown in figure 6.16.

Curve Ball

The curve ball is an effective strike ball but it is difficult to control. The ball is rolled in the same manner as the hook. At the point of release the hand is brought upward with additional lift and/or rotation. The thumb is turned from an 11 o'clock position to a 9 o'clock position. Most bowlers who throw a curve ball start from a position to the left of the center dot. The path of the ball curves toward the 1st arrow from the right hand gutter then breaks back toward the 1-3 pocket. (See figure 6.17 for path of a curve ball).

Backup Ball

The backup ball is also known as a reverse hook. It is caused by a clockwise rotation on the ball. Those who use a backup usually roll from the left side of the lane like a left hander, into the 1-2 pocket. (Fig. 6.18) The ball is held with the thumb at the 12 o'clock position. Many women throw a backup ball because of the anatomical structure of the arm. It causes the lower arm and hand to naturally angle away from the body.

If you change from a straight, curve or backup ball you may experience a drop in your average. With practice and mastery of the fundamentals of the hook you will start to exceed your previous average.

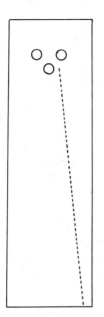

Figure 6.15. Path of straight ball.

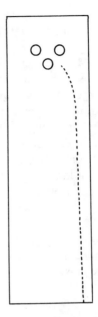

Figure 6.16. Path of hook ball.

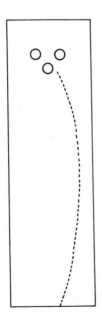

Figure 6.17. Path of curve ball.

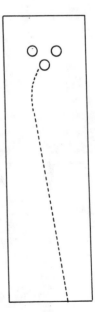

Figure 6.18. Path of backup ball.

Target Bowling

There are two basic targets to throw at in bowling, spots and pins.

Spot Bowling

Generally a spot bowler uses a target arrow as a guide to the 1-3 (strike) pocket. The 1-3 pocket is the target and the arrow is the guide to the pocket. A hook bowler generally selects the second arrow from the right hand gutter as the spot or target. Straight ball bowlers use the same spot but on more of an angle. The curve ball bowler will adjust to this spot depending upon the arch of the ball as it travels toward the pins.

The arrows don't have to be used as spots or targets. Some bowlers prefer to use a spot at the foul line or one of the spots between the foul line and the arrows. The path of the ball still rolls over the 2nd arrow from the right hand gutter.

Pin Bowling

The pin bowling method amounts to looking directly at the pins from the start of the approach to the follow through. Advocates of pin bowling believe looking further down the alley helps you throw out at the pins. This may help in getting in more lift action on the ball.

Chapter 7

The "Ballistics" of Bowling

Bowling is similar to shooting a gun. There is a "bull's eye" (the pocket), a "gun barrel" (the lane itself), a "front sight" (an arrow on the lane), a "rear sight" (the center of the shoe of the dominant foot and a dot or board on the approach), a "bullet" (the ball), and "powder" (the bowler's muscles and coordination or power that is the driving force that delivers the ball). This process is called "Ballistics."

The object of the sport of bowling is to be as consistent as possible in the "firing" or delivery of the "bullet" or ball in order to obtain high scores. Variables that cause variation in the delivery result in inconsistent and low scores. When shooting a rifle, the amount of "powder" used must be the same each time the "gun" is fired or else the "bullet" placement will vary. The same is true in bowling. The bowler must perfect the approach and release so that it is programmed to be the same each time the ball is rolled onto the lane.

Many bowlers roll the ball at one speed for strikes and at a slower speed for spares. This detracts from consistently optimal results. Each ball rolled (strike or spare) should be delivered in exactly the same manner. The only change made should be in the adjustment of the "rear sight" or right foot's position in relation to the normal strike position. This adjustment is made when moving to pick up spares or to adjust the "rear sight" foot position for lane conditions (wet or dry).

The bowler must learn to eliminate negative variables as much as possible. Start perfecting bowling by mastering the straight ball. Place the center of the right foot (all of this advice is given in terms of right handedness) on the second dot from the right side of the lane or the board that leads to the six pin. (see Fig. 5.5) Now practice rolling a straight ball over the second arrow. The four step approach should be used. When released as a straight ball, the ball should roll down the lane to the center of the six pin. Once this is mastered, ball delivery is under control or consistent. Tracking of the ball can be recorded on the sheets provided in the back of this book.

If the bowler chooses to continue rolling a straight ball, it is suggested that the right foot be placed on the second dot from the right side of the lane and walk straight toward and roll the ball over the third arrow from the right gutter. The ball should then roll straight into the 1-3 pocket. (Fig. 6.15) As an alternative, the bowler may experiment by standing with the right foot on the second spot from the left gutter. The ball is rolled into the 1-2 pocket. This gives better results for some bowlers. The starting position choice is ultimately determined by the bowler and the position that gives the best results for the bowler's individual and specific style. Experiment!

The bowler who chooses to roll a hook ball should first learn to control a straight ball. Once this is mastered (consistently rolling the ball over the second arrow into the six pin from the 2nd dot starting position), all the bowler needs to do in order to roll a hook ball is rotate the hand counterclockwise 90 degrees *after* the ball passes the right leg on the fourth or slide step of the approach. To obtain a consistent hook, the back of the right hand must be aligned with the forearm so that the fingers will be able to lift the ball from the 3 o'clock position. A wristlet helps assure consistency of proper finger location (3 o'clock) at point of release. If a wristlet is not worn, the weight of the ball will cause the wrist to break into an approximate 4:30 o'clock finger position which results in less counterclockwise rotation and a somewhat uncontrolled release.

The use of a wristlet should be considered for the serious bowler who chooses to roll a hook ball. It will make scores consistently higher by giving support and better control of the release. With the hook ball, the fingers should stay in the ball until they are pulled out by the weight of the ball. This helps give lift needed to impart the counterclockwise rotation to the ball. The hook effect is generated by this rotation.

It was mentioned earlier that mastery of the straight ball is vital to good bowling. Major errors or problems result from "shoulder drop." "Shoulder drop" may be caused by one or a combination of the following: 1) not pushing the ball away on the first step; 2) carrying the ball in front of you during the second and/or the third steps; 3) rushing the steps (the most prevalent cause of poor bowling); 4) not sliding into the release position in order to lower the shoulders and hips *together*; 5) "stork bowling" or not getting the hips down because the knees are not bent; and 6) leaning too far forward on the release.

Each of these effort or problems will cause the right shoulder to be lower than the left shoulder which causes the right hand to drift to the left. This causes the ball to roll toward the left of the target and sometimes into the left gutter. Most beginning right handed bowlers have problems with the ball going to the left because of one or a combination of the foregoing errors. The bowler should constantly self-analyze and have teammates observe one's approach and release so as to determine and help correct problems. (Use the skill drill forms in the back of this book)

Mastery of the straight ball is the most important part of ball control. If the ball misses the selected arrow (usually to its left) the bowler may still have one or more of the shoulder drop problems. If the hook ball breaks too much to the left *after* it passes properly over the center of the selected arrow the lane may be dry or the bowler is "topping" or rotating the hand counter-clockwise excessively. Rotate the hand less for less hook or not at all for the straight ball. This is an easy adjustment. In case of a dry lane, correction of excessive hook may also be helped by adjusting the right foot's starting position to the left of the normal strike position.

The major difficulty in bowling is being able to roll the center of the ball over your selected arrow consistently. Practice hitting the second arrow until control is established. Don't make the mistake of adjusting the foot "rear sight" if the ball cannot be rolled over the selected arrow; this will only compound the problem.

Remember to *slow down* the approach to allow the ball's natural pendulum swing time to take place. The left foot and right hand should be side by side during the final slide and front swing of the ball into its release on the approach. This permits good balance and control. Remember to use the same *high* follow through on every ball rolled.

Spares should be picked up with the same approach, delivery, and power that is used to roll strike balls (keep the "powder" or power consistent in the "gun"). There are three gaps or spaces between pins on each side of the head pin. The two and three pins are one gap to each side of the head pin, the four and six pins are two gaps, and the seven and ten are three gaps from the head pin. To pick up the two and eight pins (one gap or space to the left of the head pin), move two and one half boards (or inches) to the right. Now, walk *straight* to and roll the ball over the second arrow, the same as if bowling for a strike. You have adjusted your "gun's" "rear sight" to make the "bullet" go more to the left of the pocket. Move two and one half boards to the left of the strike position to pick up the three or nine pins. Move five boards (or inches) to the right to pick up the four pin, and seven and a half boards to the right to pick up the seven pin. Move five boards (or inches) to the left to pick up the six pin and seven and a half boards to the left to pick up the ten pin. Remember, for spare adjustments, walk straight to and roll the ball over the second arrow regardless of the starting position.

In moving right or left to pick up spares, the "rear sight" of the "gun" has been adjusted to make the "bullet" (the ball) go either to the left or right respectively. The "front sight" (the arrow) is not changed, only the "rear sight." Again, roll the ball exactly as though rolling for a strike. The bowlers adjustment ("2 1/2 Board Per Gap Rule") will take care of the direction or the path of the ball provided you roll the ball with your normal strike speed and style.

In "ballistic bowling," it is important to keep consistency in the game just as if shooting a gun. Try to develop a *feel* for what caused the ball to miss the target if errors are made. Remember too, that the purpose of warm-up balls is to test the condition of the lane or lanes. Be very aware of how your ball responds to the lane at this time. Adjust the starting position as needed, but keep the approach and delivery as consistent as possible. The rule of thumb is: if the ball rolls over the proper arrow but consistently misses the target, move the "rear sight" or right foot in the same direction the ball missed the target. Consistently high scores come from consistent bowling technique. This will give the bowler a base from which adjustments can be made to increase frequency of hitting the "bulls eye" with the "ballistics" of bowling!

Chapter 8

Spare Conversion

The object of the game is to knock down all the pins with each ball. It is highly improbable this will happen, even with the best bowler. In order to be a better bowler it is necessary to learn to pick up spares. There is a rule of thumb about picking up spares; use the best angle and maximum use of the alley. You want to start on the side of the approach opposite the location of the standing pins. This gives you more lane width and a better angle. This is known as bowling "cross alley". Always hit the pin nearest to you to be assured of converting the spare and not depending upon a lucky bounce. Aim the ball so it will directly strike as many pins as possible and always deliver the ball in the same manner. Spares are easier to convert than they appear. You have the width of the pin and the ball.

To convert pins on the left side (4-7-8) or any combination of these pins, the ball should be bowled across alley from right to left. You should start in the position for throwing a strike ball. Walk at a slight angle to the left. The ball should roll over the third or fourth arrow from the right hand gutter.

To convert pins left in the middle (1-2-3-5) or any combination of these pins you should start from the same position as for throwing a strike. The ball should be rolled over the second or third arrow from the right hand gutter.

Pins left on the right side of the lane (6-9-10) and any combination of these pins, you should bowl cross alley from left to right. In this starting position, the right foot is placed on the first dot to the left of the center. You should walk at a slight angle left to right toward the foul line. The ball should be rolled over the third or fourth arrow from the right gutter.

The previous three rules can be applied to convert the following common spares:

Common Spare Conversions

1-2-9

a. Throw ball from a strike position
b. Ball takes out the 1 pin and 9 pin
c. The 1 pin takes out the 2 pin
d. Hitting the 1 pin and 2 pin usually leaves the 9 pin

1-3-6-9

a. Throw from a strike position
b. Cover all pins with the ball
c. Hit head pin on right side
d. The ball carries the 1 pin, deflects, knocking down the other 3 pins

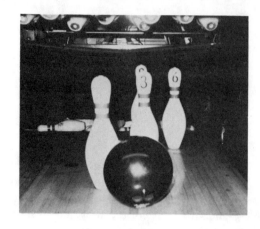

1-3-8-9

a. Throw from a strike position
b. Hit the 1 pin to the right and heavy on the 3 pin
c. The 1 pin takes out the 8 pin, the 3 pin takes out the 9 pin
d. Do not hit the 1 pin on the left side

1-2-4-7

a. Throw cross alley from a strike position
b. Hit the 1 pin on left side
c. Ball carries the other 3 pins
d. A spare can be made by hitting the 1 pin on the right
   In this case the 1 pin must knock down all the pins.

2-4-5-8

a. Throw from a strike position
b. The "bucket" must be converted by hitting the 2 pin head on
c. Ball takes out the 2, 5, & 8 pins
d. The 2 pin takes out the 4 pin
e. Hitting 2 pin light, right to left, will leave the 8 pin

3-6-10

a. Throw cross alley—left to right
b. Ball should hit the 3 pin and 6 pin
c. Deflection will carry the 10 pin
d. Don't hit the 3 pin on the left, it may cause the 6 pin to deflect around the 10 pin

3-9

a. Throw from a strike position
b. Hit both pins with the ball
c. Hitting the 3 pin on the left may cause a sliding or chopping the 3 pin off and leaving the 9 pin

3-10

  a. Throw cross alley—left to right
  b. Hit the 3 pin on the right
  c. The ball will deflect, carrying the 10 pin
  d. By hitting the 3 pin on the left the 3 pin may deflect around the 10 pin

1-2-10

  a. Throw from a strike position
  b. Hit head pin full on left side
  c. Ball covers the 2 pin
  d. The 1 pin will carry the 10 pin

5-7

  a. Throw from a strike position
  b. Hit the 5 pin on the right side
  c. The 5 pin takes out the 7 pin
  d. If the angle is too sharp, the 5 pin will miss the 7 pin

4-7-9-10

a. Throw cross alley—right to left
b. Hit 4 pin light on left side
c. Ball knocks out 7 pin
d. The 4 pin will slide over to the 9 and 10 pins

6-7-10

a. Throw cross alley—left to right
b. Hit 6 pin on extreme right side
c. Ball knocks out the 10 pin
d. The 6 pin might hit the 7 pin

4-5-7

a. Throw cross alley—right to left
b. Hit between the 4 pin and 5 pin
c. The 4 pin will take out the 7 pin

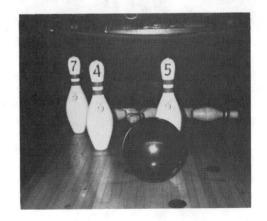

5-8-10

a. Throw cross alley—left to right
b. Hit the 5 pin to the left of center
c. The 5 pin will deflect into the 10 pin
d. The ball will carry the 8 pin

2-7

a. Throw cross alley—right to left from a strike position
b. Hit the 2 pin left of center
c. The ball will carry the 7 pin
d. Don't hit the 2 pin on the right side, it may deflect around the 7 pin

5-10

a. Throw cross alley—left to right
b. Hit the 5 pin on the left side
c. The 5 pin takes out the 10 pin
d. If the angle is too sharp, the 5 pin will miss the 10 pin

2-4-7

a. Throw cross alley—right to left from a strike position
b. Ball should hit the 2 and 4 pins
c. Deflection will carry the 7 pin
d. Don't hit the 2 pin on the right, it may cause the 4 pin to deflect around the 7 pin

Chapter 9
Analysis of Errors

Bowling involves an interrelation of many movements. In the process of refining these movements you may commit several errors. Most are done unconsciously. Most of these errors can be corrected or minimized if you are made aware of them. Many of the common errors, their causes and their remedies are presented in this chapter. Not all symptoms and/or remedies will apply to all bowlers who have a common error. In general, most errors are caused by the bowler taking his eyes off the spot when releasing the ball. Looking up may cause other errors such as improper ball release, pulling, poor follow through etc.

As you are making adjustments use the following guidelines:

Make sure of the error you are committing. If an error is only intermittent, be aware but don't be overly concerned. Errors are committed by everyone. Make sure you are working on the basic problem and not a subproblem. Only change the error, keep the other phases of the movement the same.

The following is an analysis of common errors in bowling:

COMMON ERRORS	CAUSE OF ERROR	CORRECTION
LOFTING BALL	1. Ball sticks to fingers	1. Check ball fit
	2. Standing too erect	2. Bend knees on slide and release
POOR BALANCE AT FOUL LINE	1. Leaning too far forward	1. Bend knees, keep head and shoulder up
	2. Body turned sideways	2. Walk straight, keep shoulders parallel to foul line at release
	3. Sliding foot turned	3. Point left toe straight ahead
DROPPING BALL TOO SOON	1. Poor fitting ball	1. Select a new one; Purchase your own
	2. On stance, weight is on back foot causing poor timing	2. Put weight on forward foot; start the ball moving on the first step
	3. Perspiration causes the ball to slip	3. Dry hands before taking stance, don't put fingers into ball too early
NO TIME FOR A BACKSWING	1. The push away is up and above the head	1. Push away should be out and slightly down
	2. Starting push away too late	2. Start push away simultaneously with the first step

COMMON ERRORS	CAUSE OF ERROR	CORRECTION
DRIFTING	1. Feet are pointed to side	1. When taking your stance, the feet should be pointed straight ahead
	2. The second step is away from the mid line of the body	2. The second step should be straight forward
RUNNING	1. First step too long	1. Short shuffle step on first step
	2. Incomplete arm swing	2. Add push away and increase length of the backswing
SKIDDING BALL	1. Thumb and fingers release simultaneously	1. Thumb should leave the ball first, followed by fingers
SIDE ARM THROW	1. Ball held in middle of body on horizontal axis	1. Position ball in line with right shoulder
	2. Inside-out or outisde-in swing	2. Control push away
	3. Drifting	3. Walk and slide straight toward target
LACK OF PIN ACTION	1. Affected by all other common errors listed	1. Check corrections for each error

COMMON ERRORS	CAUSE OF ERROR	CORRECTION
BALL TO RIGHT GUTTER	1. Wrap around swing	1. Use pendulum swing
	2. Released too early	2. Follow through with delivery
	3. Poor timing	3. Move up or back
	4. Dropping right shoulder	4. Keep shoulders parallel to foul line
	5. Dropping ball	5. Check weight & fit
	6. Left foot pointing to gutter	6. Point foot straight ahead
BALL TO LEFT GUTTER	1. Wrap around swing	1. Pendulum swing with elbow near body on back swing
	2. Right shoulder drop	2. Keep shoulders parallel to foul line
	3. Throwing across body	3. Pendulum swing, check follow through
ENDING ON WRONG FOOT	1. Starting on wrong foot	1. Shift weight to opposite starting foot
FOULING	1. Approach too long	1. Shorten 1st step; start back further
BALL BREAKING	1. Rotating wrist on release	1. Keep wrist and thumb in correct clock position

Chapter 10

Basic Scoring

The game of bowling consists of ten frames. The bowler is allowed two attempts if needed to knock down all 10 pins in each frame. A perfect game in bowling consists of 300 points; however, a bowler who bowls a perfect game knocks down only 120 pins. How do we arrive at a total of 300 points when only 120 pins are knocked down? The scoring system in bowling may seem rather complicated at first. The purpose of this chapter is to present the basic scoring rules in a sequential order so that a beginning bowler can easily understand the scoring system.

Scoring Terms, Symbols, and Definitions

Term: Miss or open frame

Scoring Symbol:

Definition: When a bowler fails to knock down all ten pins with two attempts.
Scoring Rule: Add the number of pins knocked down with the first ball and the number of pins knocked down with the second ball. The scoring should be 6 + 3 = 9

Term: Spare

Scoring Symbol:

Definition: All ten pins are knocked down on first and second balls. The scoring symbol indicates that 4 pins were knocked down with the first ball and 6 pins were knocked down with the second ball.
Scoring Rule: 10 points plus the number of pins knocked down with the first ball of the next frame.

Term: Strike

Scoring Symbol:

Definition: All ten pins knocked down on the first ball.
Scoring Rule: Ten points plus the total of pins knocked down with the next *two* balls rolled.

Term: Foul

Scoring Symbol:

```
 _____
| F  |__|
|    |
|____|
```

Definition: When an infraction of the rules occurs. Touching or going beyond the foul line
   is the most common foul that affects scoring.
Scoring Rule: If a foul occurs, the score for the first ball is zero. The pins are respotted and
   the second ball is rolled. If the first attempt in a frame is good and the second attempt is
   a foul, the score would be the total pins knocked down with the first ball and zero for the
   second ball.

Scoring a Complete Game

1	2	3	4	5	6	7	8	9	10	Total
6 ⌊2	8 ⟋	7 ⌊I	☒	9 ⌊—	6 ⟋	☒	4 ⌊3	☒	6⟋ 7⌋	
8	25	33	52	61	81	98	105	125	142	142

Frame by Frame Breakdown

Frame 1

```
    | 1  |
    | 6 |2 |
    |  8   |
```

This is an open frame. Six pins were knocked down with the first ball and 2 pins were knocked
down with the second ball. Eight is the total (6 + 2 = 8) for the first frame.

Frame 2

```
    | 1  | 2  |
    | 6|2 | 8|⟋ |
    |  8   |
```

Eight pins were knocked down with the first ball. A *spare* was made by knocking down the
remaining two pins with the second ball. Remember, a spare is 10 points plus the number of pins
knocked down with the first ball of the next frame. No score for the second frame can be computed
until the first ball is rolled in the third frame.

Frame 3

```
    | 1  | 2  | 3  |
    | 6|2 | 8|⟋ | 7|⌊I |
    |  8 | 25 | 33 |
```

52

Seven pins were knocked down by the first ball. You can compute the score for the second frame by adding 7 to the 10 points already scored. The second frame scored a total of 17 points (10 + 7). Now add 17 plus 8 from the first frame. The score in the second frame should be 25 (17 + 8). The third frame was an open frame. As previously mentioned, the first ball knocked down 7 pins. Add 7 to the 1 pin knocked down by the second ball. The total number of pins in the 3rd frame is 8 (7 + 1). The score in the 3rd frame is computed by adding 8 to 25. The 3rd frame score should be 33 (25 + 8).

Frame 4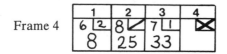

Strike. The scoring for a strike is ten points plus the total number of pins knocked down with the next two balls. The score for the 4th frame cannot be computed until the next 2 balls are rolled.

Frame 5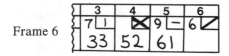

The first ball knocked down 9 pins and the second ball knocked down zero pins. First, the score for the 4th frame has to be computed. Remember, the 4th frame resulted in a strike. Therefore, the 4th frame has 10 points plus nine plus zero. (10 + 9 + 0) The total pins credited to the 4th frame is 19. To compute the 4th frame score add 19 to the previous 33 scored. The score for the 4th frame is 52. (19 + 33) The 5th frame is an open frame. Simply add 9 points to the previous 52 points (4th frame) and the 5th frame should show a total of 61 points (52 + 9).

Frame 6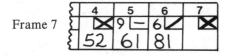

Spare. The 6th frame cannot be computed until the first ball is rolled in the next frame. Remember a spare is 10 points plus the total number of pins knocked down with the next ball.

Frame 7

4	5	6	7
☒	9 L—	6 ⮡	☒
52	61	81	

Strike. The 7th frame cannot be computed until the next 2 balls are rolled.

Frame 8

5	6	7	8
☒ 9 L—	6 ⮡	☒	4 L3
61	81	98	105

The 8th frame is an open frame. A total of 7 pins were knocked down in the 8th frame. First we have to score the 7th frame. The scoring for the strike in the 7th frame is 10 plus 7 (4 + 3). A total of 17 points (10 + 7) was scored in the 7th frame. The 17 points should be added to the previous 81 (6th frame) for a total of 98 (81 + 17). Since the 8th frame was an open frame, it can be scored immediately. Simply add 7 (4 + 3) to the previous 98 (7th frame) and you should have a total of 105 (98 + 7) for the 8th frame.

Frame 9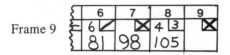

Strike. Remember a strike means 10 points plus the total number of pins knocked down with the next two balls. Frame 9 cannot be computed until the next two balls are rolled.

Frame 10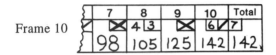

Spare. Frame 10 resulted in a spare. Scoring for a spare is 10 plus the number of pins knocked down with the next ball. In order to score frame 9 we add 10 (strike) plus 10 (spare in 10th frame for a total of 20 points in frame 9. Add 20 points to the previous score of 105 and in frame 9 we should have 125 (105 + 20). To compute frame 10, we simply add 10 to the number of pins knocked down with the next ball. The bonus ball in frame 10 knocked down 7 pins for a total of 17 points. Add 17 to the previous 125 and the score in frame 10 is 142 (125 + 17).

Key points to remember:

1. A strike means 10 points plus the total number of pins knocked down with the next two balls.
2. A spare means 10 points plus the number of pins knocked down with the next ball.

Difficult Scoring Situations

The following represent some common scoring problems that are rather confusing at first. However, if a bowler will follow the rules for scoring strikes and spares, the situation will come to be commonplace.

2 Consecutive Strikes.

Example:

1	2	3
✗	✗ 9	—
29		

To score the above example, simply remember that a strike is 10 plus the next two balls. Frame 1: Strike is 10 points plus the next ball which was 10 (strike), plus the next ball which was 9. Therefore, frame one would be 10 + 10 + 9 or 29.

3 Consecutive Strikes

Example: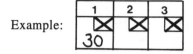

To score the above example, simply remember that a strike is 10 plus the next two balls. Frame 1: Strike is 10 points plus the next ball which was 10 (strike), plus the next ball which was 10 (strike). Therefore, frame one would be 10 + 10 + 10 or 30.

Spare then Strike

Example: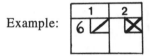

To score the above example, simply remember that a spare is 10 plus the next ball. Frame 1: Spare is 10 points plus the next ball which is a strike or 10. Therefore, frame one would be 10 + 10 or 20.

In Appendix G there are 4 hypothetical scoring assignments. Can you score all the problems correctly?

League Play

League bowling has been, and will always be, a very popular aspect of the game of bowling. A bowling team is usually composed of four or five members. Sometimes a team is composed of as few as two or three members. In competition, teams usually bowl three games per series. The team with the higher total is declared the winner.

Handicaps

In order to keep league bowling on a fair competitive basis for all teams, handicaps are established.

There are two common methods used in computing handicaps. One method is based on two-thirds the difference between the bowler's average and a score of 190.

Example:

Fred's Average	=	139
Established Average	=	190
Difference (190–139)	=	51
2/3 of Difference	=	34

Fred's handicap would be *34*

The second method of computing handicaps is by using seventy-five percent (75%) of the difference between a bowler's average and a predetermined scratch score set by the league. Usually the men's scratch score is 200, while women use 180.

Example: Fred's Average   = 139
          Scratch Score   = 200
          Difference   =   61
          Handicap (75% X 61) = 45.75

Fred's handicap would be 45 (drop all fractions)

Marks

To add interest and keep a reasonably accurate account of how a match stands, the system is a running total of each team's strikes or spares in each frame.

Each mark a team is ahead in any frame is approximately a 10-point difference, figuring strikes and spares are both worth 10 extra pins.

The following basic rules are used in figuring marks:

1. One mark is given for each spare or single strike.
2. Two marks are given for each consecutive strike.
   Exceptions:
   a. The second strike in the 10th frame is counted as one mark;
   b. Two marks are given for each consecutive strike.
3. A mark is lost if individual fails to knock over at least five pins:
   a. with the first ball following a spare;
   b. with the first ball following a multiple strike;
   c. with both balls in a frame,
   d. with both balls following a strike

Automatic Scoring

On the previous pages, steps were presented to teach the bowler the basic scoring rules in a sequential order so that a beginning bowler can easily understand the scoring system. The system taught is the manual system still used in about twenty five percent of the bowling establishments.

The age of high technology has reached the bowling industry. Most bowling establishments have installed Automatic Scoring Machines such as the one pictured below. This computerized approach simplifies record keeping for the bowling establishment as well as simplifying scoring for the bowler. Even if the bowler does not have computer skills, step-by-step instructions come directly from the TV monitor when "Left Lane" or "Right Lane" and "Help" is pressed. If necessary, help may be received from the workers at the control desk. All "Marks" and "Scoring" are automatic with this system.

Photo courtesy of AMF Bowling Inc.

Appendix A
Game Modifications

The game of bowling can be modified for class, recreational, or league play. Some common modifications include:

3,6,9 Tournament: In this game all rules of bowling are followed except every player is automatically given a strike in the third, sixth, and ninth frames. The bowler still bowls that frame but it is only for practice. It helps to improve scores and confidence.

No Tap: This game also improves scores and confidence. The regular rules of bowling are followed except that every time 1 pin remains after the 1st ball it is counted as a strike. The bowler bowls the second ball for practice.

Scotch or Dutch Doubles: This game is usually played with couples or partners. The man and woman or partners alternate balls and bowl one game together. The frames are bowled on alternate alleys as in a regular game. All rules of the regular game are observed.

One person throws the first ball and the partner tries to pick up the spare. If a strike, the partner then throws the first ball in the next frame, and continue to alternate throws.

Head Pin Tournament: The object of this game is to hit the head pin with the first ball thrown. If the head pin is hit, 10 points are scored in that frame no matter how many other pins were knocked down. There are 12 frames and the best score is 120 points. In a series of 2 games, the best score would be 360. If the head pin is not hit the score is zero for that frame. If the head pin falls from the reaction of other pins, it will not count. You must observe carefully to determine if the head pin has been hit.

Appendix B

Delivery Drill

DELIVERY DRILL

Directions: Have your bowling partner chart the path your ball traveled. See the example below
for the correct method to chart the ball path.

Name:_____ Date:_____

DELIVERY DRILL

Directions: Have your bowling partner chart the path your ball traveled. See the example below for the correct method to chart the ball path.

Name:_____ Date:_____

DELIVERY DRILL

Directions: Have your bowling partner chart the path your ball traveled. See the example below
for the correct method to chart the ball path.

Name:_____ Date:_____

DELIVERY DRILL

Directions: Have your bowling partner chart the path your ball traveled. See the example below
for the correct method to chart the ball path.

Name:_____ Date:_____

Appendix C
Head Pin Drill

HEAD PIN DRILL

Directions: Have your bowling partner mark the location of the ball as it reaches the head pin. If the headpin is knocked down, darken the circle that represents the headpin. If the headpin is missed, place an "X" in the approximate location of the ball as it reached the headpin. See the example below for the correct method of marking the head pin drill.

Name:_____ Date:_____

Example: (The ball was far right of the head pin)

HEAD PIN DRILL

Directions: Have your bowling partner mark the location of the ball as it reaches the head pin. If the headpin is knocked down, darken the circle that represents the headpin. If the headpin is missed, place an "X" in the approximate location of the ball as it reached the headpin. See the example below for the correct method of marking the head pin drill.

Name:_____   Date:_____

Example: (The ball was far right of the head pin)

HEAD PIN DRILL

Directions: Have your bowling partner mark the location of the ball as it reaches the head pin. If the headpin is knocked down, darken the circle that represents the headpin. If the headpin is missed, place an "X" in the approximate location of the ball as it reached the headpin. See the example below for the correct method of marking the head pin drill.

Name:_____ Date:_____

Example: (The ball was far right of the head pin)

HEAD PIN DRILL

Directions: Have your bowling partner mark the location of the ball as it reaches the head pin. If the headpin is knocked down, darken the circle that represents the headpin. If the headpin is missed, place an "X" in the approximate location of the ball as it reached the headpin. See the example below for the correct method of marking the head pin drill.

Name:_____ Date:_____

Example: (The ball was far right of the head pin)

Appendix D
7 Pin Drill

7 PIN DRILL

Directions: Have your bowling partner mark the location of the ball as it reached the 7 pin area. If the 7 pin is knocked down, darken the circle representing the 7 pin. If the 7 pin is missed, place an "X" in the approximate location of the ball as it reached the 7 pin area. See the example below for the correct method of marking the 7 pin drill.

Name:_____ Date:_____

Example: (The ball was rolled slightly to the right of the seven pin)

7 PIN DRILL

Directions: Have your bowling partner mark the location of the ball as it reached the 7 pin area.
If the 7 pin is knocked down, darken the circle representing the 7 pin. If the 7 pin is
missed, place an "X" in the approximate location of the ball as it reached the 7 pin
area. See the example below for the correct method of marking the 7 pin drill.

Name:_____ Date:_____

Example: (The ball was rolled slightly to the right of the seven pin)

7 PIN DRILL

Directions: Have your bowling partner mark the location of the ball as it reached the 7 pin area. If the 7 pin is knocked down, darken the circle representing the 7 pin. If the 7 pin is missed, place an "X" in the approximate location of the ball as it reached the 7 pin area. See the example below for the correct method of marking the 7 pin drill.

Name:_____ Date:_____

Example: (The ball was rolled slightly to the right of the seven pin)

7 PIN DRILL

Directions: Have your bowling partner mark the location of the ball as it reached the 7 pin area. If the 7 pin is knocked down, darken the circle representing the 7 pin. If the 7 pin is missed, place an "X" in the approximate location of the ball as it reached the 7 pin area. See the example below for the correct method of marking the 7 pin drill.

Name:_____ Date:_____

Example: (The ball was rolled slightly to the right of the seven pin)

Appendix E
10 Pin Drill

10 PIN DRILL

Directions: Have your bowling partner mark the location of the ball as it reaches the 10 pin area. if the 10 pin is knocked down, darken the circle representing the 10 pin. If the 10 pin is missed, place an "X" in the approximate location of the ball as it reached the 10 pin area. See the example below for the correct method of marking the 10 pin drill.

Name:_____ Date:_____

Example: (The ball knocked down the 10 pin)

10 PIN DRILL

Directions: Have your bowling partner mark the location of the ball as it reaches the 10 pin area. if the 10 pin is knocked down, darken the circle representing the 10 pin. If the 10 pin is missed, place an "X" in the approximate location of the ball as it reached the 10 pin area. See the example below for the correct method of marking the 10 pin drill.

Name:_____ Date:_____

Example: (The ball knocked down the 10 pin)

10 PIN DRILL

Directions: Have your bowling partner mark the location of the ball as it reaches the 10 pin area. if the 10 pin is knocked down, darken the circle representing the 10 pin. If the 10 pin is missed, place an "X" in the approximate location of the ball as it reached the 10 pin area. See the example below for the correct method of marking the 10 pin drill.

Name:_____ Date:_____

Example: (The ball knocked down the 10 pin)

10 PIN DRILL

Directions: Have your bowling partner mark the location of the ball as it reaches the 10 pin area. if the 10 pin is knocked down, darken the circle representing the 10 pin. If the 10 pin is missed, place an "X" in the approximate location of the ball as it reached the 10 pin area. See the example below for the correct method of marking the 10 pin drill.

Name:_____ Date:_____

Example: (The ball knocked down the 10 pin)

Appendix F

Individual Progress Sheet

INDIVIDUAL PROGRESS SHEET

DATE	1ST GAME	2ND GAME	3RD GAME	SERIES TOTAL	AVERAGE

Appendix G

Scoring Assignments

SCORING ASSIGNMENT #1

1	2	3	4	5	6	7	8	9	10	
7 1	2 6	9 —	3 4	8 /	5 2	7 1	3 2	4 4	3 6	

1	2	3	4	5	6	7	8	9	10	
8 —	4 /	7 2	3 5	4 5	6 /	7 1	8 —	4 3	— 7	

1	2	3	4	5	6	7	8	9	10	
9 /	7 —	4 3	2 7	6 /	8 —	9 /	9 —	6 /	4 2	

1	2	3	4	5	6	7	8	9	10	
7 —	9 /	7 /	4 —	9 —	5 /	2 7	6 —	9 /	9 —	

1	2	3	4	5	6	7	8	9	10	
X	7 1	9 —	2 5	— 9	6 /	7 /	9 —	4 3	2 / 6	

SCORING ASSIGNMENT #2

1	2	3	4	5	6	7	8	9	10	
8 −	9 /	7 ⌊2	9 /	− ⌊4	☒	7 ⌊2	☒	4 /	⌊6⌉3	

1	2	3	4	5	6	7	8	9	10	
☒	2 ⌊7	4 /	9 /	7 −	1 ⌊8	3 /	9 −	4 ⌊5	⌊7⌉/ 7	

1	2	3	4	5	6	7	8	9	10	
− /	☒	4 ⌊5	3 ⌊1	8 ⌊1	☒	7 ⌊2	6 ⌊2	☒	− ⌊8	

1	2	3	4	5	6	7	8	9	10	
9 −	4 ⌊5	6 −	7 /	☒	8 ⌊1	9 /	8 ⌊1	4 /	⌊7⌉−	

1	2	3	4	5	6	7	8	9	10	
8 ⌊1	7 /	7 ⌊2	1 ⌊3	☒	3 ⌊6	4 /	☒	7 /	⌊2⌉6	

SCORING ASSIGNMENT #3

1	2	3	4	5	6	7	8	9	10	
⊠ 6 ⟋	– ⎿7	8 ⟋	7 ⟋	9 ⟋	4 ⎿2	9 –	4 ⟋	⎿6⟋	9	

1	2	3	4	5	6	7	8	9	10	
9 –	⊠	⊠ 7 ⎿2	6 ⟋	9 ⟋	⊠	5 –	3 ⟋	⊠ 7	1	

1	2	3	4	5	6	7	8	9	10	
F 6 – ⎿5	⊠ 9 –	6 ⎿3	9 –	4 ⎿5	– ⟋	⊠	⊠ 6 3			

1	2	3	4	5	6	7	8	9	10	
9 ⟋	⊠ – ⟋	6 F	9 –	4 ⟋	5 ⟋	7 ⟋	⊠	⎿6⟋	4	

1	2	3	4	5	6	7	8	9	10	
⊠ 9 –	⊠ – ⎿7	6 ⎿3	2 ⎿4	⊠ 7 ⎿2	6 2	⊠⊠ 4				

SCORING ASSIGNMENT #4

Sample Bowling Test

TRUE OR FALSE:

1. A bowling game consists of 10 frames.
2. The most points a bowler can score in any one frame is 30.
3. A strike in the tenth frame entitles the bowler to two more balls.
4. To roll a perfect game, the bowler must have ten strikes.
5. If bowlers on adjoining lanes are ready to start their approach at the same time, the bowler on the right is given the courtesy of bowling first.
6. On the four step approach, the fourth step is more of a slide than a step and is longer than the three previous steps.
7. If the first step of the approach is taken simultaneously with the push-away forward motion of the ball, the next three steps should coincide with the arm swing action in rhythmic sequence.
8. If a bowler touches the lane beyond the foul line on his/her first delivery, he/she loses score of both rolls.
9. The position of the hand for the hook delivery for a right handed bowler is "thumb at 10-11 fingers at 4–5."
10. A ball hitting to the left of the headpin (1-2 pocket) for right-handed bowlers is called a Brooklyn.
11. The straight ball delivery requires less hand and wrist strength than the hook ball delivery.
12. The letters A.B.C. refer to the national bowling organization call the Allied Bowling Congress.
13. The finger holes for the "straight ball" should be approximately six-o'clock.
14. Men bowlers and the majority of women bowlers should learn the hook delivery at the very beginning of class.
15. In the four-step delivery the ball-is pushed away from the body on the second step.
16. Between rolls of the two balls, the bowler should step to the rear of the approach.
17. In delivering a hook ball, the bowler should feel the thumb release first, then the fingers.
18. For the proper starting position in the four-step approach, most of the body weight is on the right foot to act as a reminder that the first step should be taken on the left foot.
19. On the four-step approach, the first three steps should be longer than the 4th step.
20. When a player fouls, no score is allowed on the ball.
21. An A.B.C. approved pin is 15" high.
22. Pins are 3 ft. apart from center to center.
23. The length of the approach is 15' and the length of the lane is 75'.
24. Bowling was originally called Kegling.
25. Arrows are targets imbedded in the lane to help a player align the starting position on the approach with the ball path to the pocket.
26. A backup ball for a right-handed bowler starts out to the right then curves back to the left.
27. Knocking down the front pin of a spare and leaving the other pins standing is called a chop or cherry.
28. The most important fundamental of bowling is the push away.

29. A dead ball is a poorly rolled ball that has little or no spin or "action" and doesn't knock down as many pins as it should.
30. An error is also known as a blow, miss or open.
31. The 2 4-5-8 pin leave is called baby split.
32. The area behind the Foul Line is called the approach.
33. The king pin is the #1 pin.
34. A creeper is a pin hidden behind another.
35. A water ball is a poorly delivered ball.
36. The last bowler on a team is the backup.
37. The 4-9 split is called a bedpost.
38. The Lead Off is the first bowler on a team.
39. The 5 7 pin leave is a sour apple.
40. A Series is usually three games or more.
41. A grinder is a powerful hook or curve ball.
42. A graveyard means the angle at which the holes are bored in a ball.
43. A Convert is a game under 200, actually between 100 and 200.
44. A Double is a powerful hook or curve ball.
45. A Railroad is a 1-2-4-10 pin leave for a right-hander.
46. 100 pins are knocked down in a perfect 300 game.
47. The number 5 pin is called the Head Pin.
48. A Deuce means the same as a crossover.
49. A Sleeper is a ball rolled very slowly.
50. The fewest number of balls that can be rolled in a complete game is 20.

Answers to Sample Bowling Test

1.	T	26.	F
2.	T	27.	T
3.	T	28.	T
4.	F	29.	T
5.	T	30.	T
6.	T	31.	F
7.	T	32.	T
8.	F	33.	F
9.	T	34.	F
10.	T	35.	T
11.	T	36.	F
12.	F	37.	F
13.	T	38.	T
14.	F	39.	T
15.	F	40.	T
16.	T	41.	T
17.	T	42.	F
18.	F	43.	F
19.	F	44.	F
20.	T	45.	F
21.	T	46.	F
22.	F	47.	F
23.	F	48.	F
24.	T	49.	F
25.	T	50.	F

Selected References

ABC. *Playing Rules*, 1980-81.

ABC, WIBC. *Bowler's Guide*, 1979.

Corbin, Charles B., et al. *Concepts In Physical Education*, William C. Brown Company Publishers, 1981.

WIBC. *Bowling Etiquette*

WIBC. *Foul Rules*